A Flamboyance of Flamingos

by

SALLY KING

Illustrated by: Corinna Holyoake

A Collection of Birds

Reading in Rhyme
A Flamboyance of Flamingos

26 COLLECTIVE NOUNS FOR GROUPS OF BIRDS
INCORPORATED INTO RHYME

This book is published by
Grosvenor House Publishing Ltd
Link House
140 The Broadway, Tolworth, Surrey, KT6 7HT.
www.grosvenorhousepublishing.co.uk

A CIP record for this book
is available from the British Library

ISBN 978-1-78623-455-1

CONTENTS

A BELLOW OF BULLFINCHES

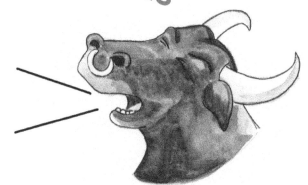

Pretty birds with bright pink breast.
We know this is the male.
Feeding on insects, buds and flowers,
A flash of black cap and tail.

We know he is here by that mournful call,
His sad note, his cry,
Not the BELLOW of the sturdy bull,
Strong and still in the field nearby.

Maybe the bull in his name gives a clue,
For, yes, bulls are said to bellow.
But a sorrowful note is all we hear
From this colourful little fellow.

A BELLOW OF BULLFINCHES,
three or four of these birds,
It's a strange term to learn somehow,
Not a flash, a flight, but a BELLOW
When we see a group of them now.

A BEVY OF LARKS

Larks are songbirds and they sing
At daybreak, a morning call,
Such a melodious, elaborate song,
It gladdens the hearts of us all.

Used in the past to signify
Religion and true love,
The lark, an unassuming bird,
Is gentle, like the dove.

A BEVY, a large group
Of anything, person or bird,
Is an ordinary term for a bird that creates
The most beautiful call you have heard.

A BEVY OF LARKS is rare to see,
Yet, they make such a haunting sound,
The morning lark, mentioned in music and art,
In literature also is found.

That rapturous sound breaks through the dawn
And lifts the rising sun,
A BEVY OF LARKS brings joy to our hearts
And announces that day has begun.

A BOUQUET OF PHEASANTS

A bouquet of flowers brings colour to mind,
A BOUQUET OF PHEASANTS is just as kind,
For the male pheasant is a bird of beauty,
His iridescent colours make it our duty
To protect him.

Colours of copper, gold, purple, red,
A long, long tail and mottled head,
Introduced by the Normans it's said, for sport,
Maybe from China, another thought.
We welcome this bird to stay.

He is a symbol of our land,
Our countryside, you understand,
The far-crying call
Recognised by us all,
This gamebird bred for sporting.

A BOUQUET OF PHEASANTS

They come with their guns, dressed in countryside green,
From Autumn to Spring the shoots can be seen,
Congregating for sport and pleasure,
Using their well earned hours of leisure
To win a brace or two.

Hidden amongst the ferns and grasses,
A display of colour suddenly flashes,
As you walk past and startle the male,
Up he flies, gilded wings and tail,
With that call of distress and warning.

To watch two males confront and fight,
Defending their territory by right,
Is a BOUQUET of colour! A true display!
Both determined that both will stay,
And determined for both to survive.

A CAST OF FALCONS

Falcons are truly amazing birds,
They fly on their tapered wings,
Their diving speed is unsurpassed
Amongst other things.

The falcon is a bird of prey,
Hunting through the skies,
It spots its kill from miles away
And dives to grab its prize.

It is diurnal, hunts through the day,
With vision that will astound,
Then, in a dive, the fastest bird
For many miles around.

Perhaps the noun derives from this.
For a shadow is cast in flight,
Almost menacing overhead
A dark CAST, as black as night.

When seen in groups on cliff tops high,
They are called A CAST indeed.
A CAST OF FALCONS, that's what we say.
Nothing can beat their speed.

A CHARM OF FINCHES

"A bellow of bullfinches" has already been said,
But goldfinches are a CHARM,
A bright red face, yellow patch on wings,
Sweet and dainty, they wish you no harm.

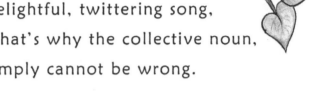

Charming birds with a liquid call,
A delightful, twittering song,
Perhaps that's why the collective noun,
Simply cannot be wrong.

They live near thistles and seeded plants,
On heathland, a common, a moor,
They visit your bird tables, gardens or parks,
Seen in groups of three or four.

So, next time you see them, say "There's a CHARM!
A CHARM OF FINCHES, it's true,"
Sweetest of birds, spectacular plumage,
Red, black and intense yellow hue.

A CLATTERING OF JACKDAWS

Jackdaws are a form of Crow,
Raven and Jay, both are cousins, you know.

Intelligent and social, they pick up tricks,
They build their nests simply out of sticks.

Then line them with wool carried in the bill.
Jackdaws eat roadside kill

And sometimes eggs from another bird,
Carrion creatures or so I have heard.

And when a group rests in a tree,
A CLATTERING OF JACKDAWS is what you'll see.

The noise "Jack-Jack" is very near,
And CLATTERING is perfect for the clatter we hear.

This small, black crow, with tiny eyes
Roosts high with rooks and joins their cries.

Magpies, jays and ravens too,
All create the same ado.

This noise and commotion! Your friends you can tell,
The collective noun CLATTER suits very well.

A CONVOCATION OF EAGLES

The eagle has been called the King of Birds,
The largest bird of prey,
With keen eyesight and powerful wings
That lead him on his way.

A fierce hooked beak, sharp talons too,
He nests in trees up high,
On top of cliffs, an eyrie fine,
Soaring to the sky.

An assembly of people is a CONVOCATION,
A group of eagles the same,
A CONVOCATION OF EAGLES you know,
That is the collective name.

The eagle glides high over the hills,
Favours islands, a Scottish glen,
Often solitary, sometimes seen in a pair,
But in very cold weather, it's then...

They perch together to keep themselves warm,
Sleeping through much of the night,
It's when you see groups huddled together,
A CONVOCATION,
a gathering, is right.

A COVERT OF COOTS

They patter across the water surface
With a shield above the white beak,
Found on lakes or in gravel pits,
Black feathers, silky and sleek.

A cousin of moorhens, they're noisy birds,
They can be seen all the year round,
Eating vegetation, insects, water snails,
Sometimes pecking on the ground.

A COVERT seems a misnomer,
For such an aggressive little bird,
Not shy, he needs no secret thicket
To hide and not be heard.

His metallic call can be loud and harsh,
His eyes a scarlet red,
A pale pink beak, white tipped wings,
That white shield upon his head.

Taking off from the water, they "spatter" across
The surface and look so absurd!
A COVERT OF COOTS is the name we give
To these characterful water birds.

A COVEY OF GROUSE

A COVEY is a small group of birds.
Which describes us very well.
We live amongst heather, in woodland too,
Many in Highland fell.
Red grouse or black, we nest on the ground,
In shallow depressions quite low,
Black grouse can be pretty with feathered toes
To help us walk on the snow.
The males fan out their tails for effect,
A marvellous sight to behold,
Millions are bred for the shooting men,
Gamebirds, like partridge, I'm told.
So A COVEY OF GROUSE in Scotland you'll see,
Amongst heathers where we are sat,
Something you might glimpse, if you visit the town,
Is a tail feather worn in a hat!

A DESCENT OF WOODPECKERS

Woodpeckers always make me laugh
The way they hang on wood.
Tree trunks. Telegraph poles. Peck! Peck! Peck!
Grabbing insects as they should.

Vertically hanging, toes facing both ways,
In order to brace and grip,
They climb up and down from very great height
A DESCENT OF WOODPECKERS won't slip.

Constantly drumming and beating on wood,
But from headaches they never suffer,
For their little skulls are reinforced
And act completely as a buffer.

Isn't Nature wonderful? Amazing adaptation.
That flash of colour we love,
That chirp, the chatter, the Peck! Peck! Peck!
That DESCENT of birds from above

A PARLIAMENT OF OWLS

An owl is a solitary creature,
Strange then, they have a collective name,
"As wise as an owl" may be of some help,
For a government purports the same.

The group name is PARLIAMENT,
The highest legislature,
A PARLIAMENT OF OWLS and government
May have a connection, for sure.

An owl has acute hearing,
His soft edged wings in flight
Make him a silent predator,
Swooping for prey at night.

His hoots and night time screeches,
Can leave a haunting impression,
So if you do see two or more owls,
Then a PARLIAMENT could be in session.

A FLAMBOYANCE OF FLAMINGOS

Tropical wading birds with backward bending knees,
Stir up mud with their feet, messy if you please.

Flamingos attract attention, of that there is no doubt,
But pink in colour? How and what can that be all about?

On crustaceans they are known to dine, from a shallow pool,
Which turn their feathers shades of pink, as a general rule.

A FLAMBOYANCE OF FLAMINGOS

Flamboyant then, the word, it does describe them well,
A very special species we can for certain tell.

Known for a flamingo-flamenco dance,
Heads move in a sort of mystical trance.

Tall and pink, a huge flock will leave a strong impression,
Deserving of their collective name, its hint of alliteration.

"A FLAMBOYANCE OF FLAMINGOS." Such appropriate words
For flocks of these sometimes comical, but very beautiful birds.

A FLIGHT OF DOVES

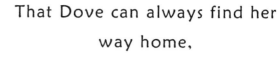

A symbol of peace, the dove,
Can also be a symbol of love.

Gentle doves, who sleep,
Heads between shoulders,
not a peep.

Until they pick grains from the
ground,
Without a sound.

Just a gentle "coo".
A pigeon is in the family too.

Though doves are smaller with
longer tails,
To astonish us, it never fails,

That Dove can always find her
way home,
Over hundreds of miles, all alone.

She has been used to message
during war,
Trained to fly back to her place
before.

So the collective term, A FLIGHT,
Seems to be so very right.

A PARTY OF JAYS

"Let's have a party!" we hear the jays cry,
Acorn eaters, with a loud shout,
But, really, these birds are terribly shy,
They're just letting you know they're about.

Related to jackdaw, magpie and crow,
The jay is colourful and bright,
Feathers are taken for fly fishing you know,
Pink, striking blue, black and white.

A PARTY OF JAYS overhead may hover,
And they can make a great deal of sound,
But rarely moving from woodland cover,
They cannot always be found.

So where have they gone?
You may hear someone say,
Well, they're having a bash,
A PARTY today!

A GANG OF TURKEYS

Turkeys need to be in a gang,
They stress if left alone,
So A GANG OF TURKEYS works quite well,
Within a turkey zone.

They can be aggressive creatures,
Bully boys en masse,
Fairly frightening if you're an alien
The gang will not let pass.

Turkeys are known to spar and fight,
Strutting with puffed out breast,
So be wary of this GANG of birds,
They'll put you to the test.

The male sports a snood and wattle
Both over and under his beak,
Bred mainly for meat on special occasions,
Thanksgiving or Christmas week.

Turkeys hate to be alone,
Perch together upon a straw bale,
A stranger invading the group will be
Attacked, aggressively, without fail.

So A GANG OF TURKEYS you might say
Is a suitable name for the breed,
Beware of invading turkey space
Or you may be sorry indeed.

A GANG OF TURKEYS

A GULP OF CORMORANTS

The cormorant, a long necked water bird,
With broad wings and quite a large tail.
On rocky shores and coastal sites
You will spot him without fail.

In a group together we call them a GULP,
Perhaps due to the way they eat.
They have large bills to catch their fish
And four toes on big webbed feet.

So when you see a collection of these,
Down by the sea one day,
You can use the proper collective noun,
A GULP is what you'll say.

Their nests are seaweed, reeds and twigs,
And in colonies they survive,
Their black plumage, not naturally waterproof,
Enables a very deep dive.

These birds can be very greedy,
Stealing a fisherman's catch,
Gulping it down and storing it
For when the baby chicks hatch.

Then with a gulp it comes up again
To feed the young chicks in the nest,
So A GULP OF CORMORANTS seems a good name
In this collective noun quest.

A GULP OF CORMORANTS

A LAMENTATION OF SWANS

Pure white plumage and long, curved neck,
A stately swan glides by,
A flying bird, revered by many,
So LAMENTATION begs the question, Why?

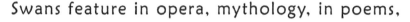

A LAMENTATION is deep grief and sorrow,
Intense, heartfelt cries,
"The swan song" may derive from such,
For Mute Swan sings before she dies.

Swans feature in opera, mythology, in poems,
And in stories from far and wide,
Denmark has made it the national bird,
Their author created great pride.

His tale of The Ugly Duckling,
Their national bird based upon,
Written by H. C. Andersen,
A grey cygnet became a fine swan.

Herbivorous, dabbling in the reeds,
By water, swans build their nests,
Aggressively protective
From all invading pests.

A symbol of love and fidelity
To their partners, their daughters, their sons,
Such characteristics linger in our minds,
Truly, the LAMENTATION OF SWANS.

A MURDER OF CROWS

Crows are clever birds. Quite fearless,
Seen alone or as a pair,
Feeding on any scraps they can,
Unafraid, they swoop without care.

When we see them in a group,
Perched on a wire or a fence,
Noisy creatures, ugly, black and large,
The name A MURDER makes some sense.

For occasionally a crow will kill
Another crow, its own kind,
Or feed on carcasses of its own dead friends,
Anything it can find.

To farmers they are constant pests,
Stealing their seedlings and their crops,
For protection they roost in large numbers,
Social, but noisy, in the tree tops.

Crows may be frightening to some,
With their feathers as black as granite,
But actually they are very smart birds,
The cleverest on our planet.

A MURDER OF CROWS is what we say,
When a collection of crows is around,
Jackdaws and magpies, the same family groups,
But A MURDER OF CROWS you have found.

A MURMURATION OF STARLINGS

At a feeding station
Black and noisy might be seen,
But take a closer look,
Glossy sheens of purple and green.

Chatty, gregarious birds,
Bullies, their greed a recognised sin,
Autumn chill descending,
And the murmuring ballets begin.

Surging, rising, at dusk,
Beneath a watery, setting sun,
The mass of beating wings.
A MURMURATION has begun.

Connected together,
Twisting and turning in their flight,
Filling the sky above us.
A magnificent, breathtaking sight.

Coordinated patterns,
Hundreds and thousands dance together,
Wheeling, spinning above us
In the cold and wintry weather.

Then dropping down to roost
Over piers, reed beds and trees,
Murmur at last is silenced,
The completed drama, at ease.

A MURMURATION OF STARLINGS

A MUSTER OF PEACOCKS
or
AN OSTENTATION OF PEACOCKS

Peacocks are a breed
Of large, colourful pheasants in need
Of space to strut, parade and roost,
A country park or stately home might host
These beautiful creatures.

The male is the king of drama.
His wife is very much calmer.
He sports a magnificent fan
Of a tail, and he can
Command a great audience.

Iridescent feathers of blue, gold, red,
With white eyespots, outspread,
He calls in early morning
And late evening, without warning,
This national bird of India.

A MUSTER does not seem worthy for
Such a gathering. It seems a poor
Comparison with "mustering a troop"
But it's necessary to stoop
To the collective term we are given.

So it is A MUSTER OF PEACOCKS, but wait!
OSTENTATION suits better, it's not too late!
The showy display, a perfect definition,
So, let us be granted fresh permission.
To call them AN OSTENTATION too!

A MUSTER OF PEACOCKS
or
AN OSTENTATION OF PEACOCKS

A PANDEMONIUM OF PARROTS

Chaos and craziness ensue
If you have a parrot and a cockatoo,
Along with budgerigar, macaw,
You may as well add a few more,
The parakeet, the parrotlet, the lory,
And in my fury
Let me add a lovebird and a kakapo.
Hundreds of species, don't you know.
A PANDEMONIUM OF PARROTS it will be
With screams and chatter all around me.
Tropical birds with colours vivid and bright,
Except cockatoo who is mainly white.
The rest are predominately green,
Although red, blue and yellow can be seen.

A PANDEMONIUM OF PARROTS

A distinguishing feature is very strong feet
Used by both parrot and parakeet
For climbing and swinging,
Sometimes bringing
The food that they eat
Sometimes savoury, sometimes sweet,
Manipulated, used like human hands,
Here the parrot stands
And cracks open a nut
In his strong, curved bill, but
He also eats seeds and he fools
Us by using particular tools
And imitating human speech
So cleverly. He can even reach
A puzzle and solve it.
What reasoning and wit
We must attribute to this bird.
How absurd!

A PANDEMONIUM OF PARROTS makes sense,
To acknowledge all that powerful intelligence!

A RAFT OF DUCKS

We all know a duck and a drake
Dabbling together upon the lake.

But a group of ducks is known as a RAFT.
I know what you're saying. You think I'm daft.

A RAFT OF DUCKS is what we say
When we see them together and we stay...

To look at their waterproof feathers spread
As they preen themselves, swim or make a bed.

A nest by the river, pond or lake,
The female duck the noise will make,

The grunt, the chirp, the quack,
But let's get back

To THE RAFT OF DUCKS,
birds of a feather,
The collection of ducks sitting together

When on the water, a landing craft,
Maybe the group together looks like a raft.

A RAFT OF DUCKS, the collective noun,
For the group together settling down.

A RASP OF GUINEA FOWL

Birds from Africa, we don't like the cold,
For we nest on the ground in flocks,
We prefer living in groups in wide open spaces
To having a coop with a nesting box.

Sometimes mistaken for turkeys or partridge,
We have featherless heads with crests,
We can run very fast and fly very high,
We keep down your insects and pests.

We are chatty and loud, good at guarding your home,
For we don't like intruders at all,
Together we're known as "A RASP OF GUINEA FOWL",
Probably something to do with our call.

The noise we make can annoy your neighbours,
We screech from dawn until the day ends,
"A RASP OF GUINEA FOWL" is not to be kept
If you want your neighbours as friends!

A SEDGE OF CRANES

A crane is a stork-like bird, unrelated to heron, I think,
Not a lifting machine. The spelling does create a link.

Long legs, broad wings, so they fly far away,
They migrate in Winter, return April or May.

The sedge is a grass-like plant we find
Often in very wet places,
So maybe the word fits a collection like this,
As cranes prefer wetland spaces.

These migrating birds come back in the Spring
So we need a collective noun,
The fantastic sight of the group overhead,
Is A SEDGE OF CRANES coming down.

Huge and graceful, long neck and legs,
With a lengthy, amplified call,
Gathering in large flocks to feed and nest,
They stand majestic and tall.

Symbolic birds in many cultures,
Featuring in dance and mime,
The subject of fables, poetry, Kung-Fu moves,
Cranes date back to an ancient time.

A SEDGE OF CRANES

As symbols of happiness, eternal youth,
Vigilance, or bird of omen,
A celebration of life, or a symbol of peace,
Seen in origami from Japan.

Grace and beauty define these birds,
In movement, flock or flight,
A group is a SEDGE, a HERD, or a DANCE.
All of these words would be right.

AN UNKINDNESS OF RAVENS

Six ravens guard the Tower of London,
Or the monarchy will fall.
These ravens can imitate human speech,
But a distinctive croak is their call.

AN UNKINDNESS OF RAVENS
might be apt in some ways,
For in this Bloody Tower,
Many unkindnesses have been done,
Acts that would make you cower.

Ravens have long been associated with death,
And are included in myths and fable,
They are highly intelligent, mimic and play,
And scavenge food from wherever they are
able.

Teenage ravens join up in gangs,
This is a mother's worst nightmare,
But to call a group AN UNKINDNESS,
Might not always be totally fair.

For ravens know whom they like and want as their friends,
They will console and show empathy, I've heard,
They play with toys and know how to have fun,
More like a puppy than a huge bird.

AN UNKINDNESS OF RAVENS

The UNKINDNESS OF RAVENS may have derived
From a legend long ago,
Which tells that their young are pushed out of the nest,
So maybe the name fits them so.

A WAKE OF VULTURES

Naked neck, hunched stance, featherless scalp,
Easy to malign,
Bald, ugly, squabbling birds,
On dead carcasses they dine.

A WAKE is a vigil beside the dead,
So A WAKE OF VULTURES is apt of course,
They sit and wait in a shifty way.
Scavengers. What could be worse?

But have you seen a vulture fly?
Gliding, thermally soaring?
Biological waste controllers,
We don't need dead carcasses storing.

So a group of vultures we call a WAKE,
It all looks somewhat primeval,
Try to see A WAKE OF VULTURES,
As a necessary evil.

COLLECTIVE NOUNS FOR COLLECTIONS OF BIRDS

So, we have reached the end of these little verses,
All of which you have, hopefully, read.
Did you learn some new words for groups of these birds?
Or has it all just gone over your head?

Which one was your favourite?
Or which did you hate?
Which scored a zero?
And which did you rate?

Whatever you thought,
Let's hope it was fun,
Perhaps educational?
Your friends you can stun.

All this vocabulary
Now stored in your brain,
You can quote to your friends
Again and again.

A group of doves is a flight,
Owls hunt at night,

Jackdaws are brainy,
Parrots are zany,

Simply swans altogether,
Elegant, white of feather,

Become a lamentation,
Peacocks, an ostentation.

Collective nouns for birds,
It's called "the joy of words".

Lightning Source UK Ltd.
Milton Keynes UK
UKHW052211160821
388812UK00002B/93